Guffaws in Grief: A Hilarious Handbook for Healing

Ana Paula McCulloch

Contents

Introduction

Jim, a multifaceted individual, embraced diverse roles such as a dedicated milk delivery man, adept computer builder, skilled boxer, war veteran, and ultimately, a remarkable engineer. His brilliant mind extended to even the calculation of today's date, a month that held profound significance – the month of our marriage, his mother's birthday, and my parents' wedding anniversary. September, forever etched in memory, will never be forgotten.

A decade of shared experiences unfolded within the rich tapestry of our lives. Our unconventional family, consisting of two chickens, a parrot, and a loyal dog, weathered storms both literal and metaphorical during our extensive seafaring adventures. From enduring pirate attacks to navigating treacherous waves, we forged enduring memories.

Our journey spanned the seven continents, from Antarctica's penguin colonies to Venice's canals. Riding camels, donkeys, elephants, and horses, we explored the pyramids of Egypt, swam in idyllic beaches from Ibiza to the Caribbean, and witnessed the grandeur of historical landmarks such as the Colosseum, the Wailing Wall in Jerusalem, and Notre Dame in France. From the towering mountains of Norway to the mosques of Istanbul, we immersed ourselves in diverse cultures.

Our adventures continued through the stone city of Jordan, a ride on a chuck chuck in Sri Lanka, hearing the Big Ben bell, sailing the Amazon River, dancing with indigenous tribes, and celebrating the Day of Los Muertos in Mexico. Dining on the 122nd floor of the Burj Khalifa in Dubai and exploring the Rocinha favela were among the countless unforgettable experiences. Our journey reached its pinnacle at the End of the World in Ushuaia.

Now, as the cruise concludes for you, Jim, the journey continues for me, propelled by the winds of cherished memories and the love that echoes through time.

Guffaws in Grief: A Hilarious Handbook for Healing

Ana Paula McCulloch

In loving memory of my dear husband, Jim (James Ian McCulloch), who departed from this world far too soon, at the tender age of 39. He lived a life filled with passion, embodying qualities of fairness, diligence, honesty, and an infectious sense of humor. Jim was, without a doubt, the most generous soul I've ever had the privilege of knowing. My love for you knows no bounds, darling, and the void left by your absence is keenly felt.

Chapter 1

Welcome, dear reader, to a place where tears and laughter share the same stage, where the weight of grief meets the levity of laughter. In this peculiar corner of coping, we embark on a journey through the uncharted territory of humor in the face of loss.

Grief is a journey that takes us through a myriad of emotions – sorrow, anger, confusion, and, yes, even moments of unexpected hilarity. The Laughter Lounge of Loss is not a dismissal of the pain that accompanies grief; rather, it's an exploration of the healing power found within the folds of humor.

Why a laughter lounge, you might ask? Because, my friend, sometimes life hands us a script that's equal parts tragedy and comedy. As we navigate the complexities of loss, we'll discover that laughter can be a faithful companion on this rollercoaster ride. It's not about making light of our struggles, but about finding the light within them.

Throughout the pages that follow, we'll explore how humor can be a coping mechanism, a release valve for the pent-up emotions, and a source of strength when the world seems heavy. So, fasten your seatbelt, loosen your tie, or kick off your shoes – whatever makes you comfortable – as we venture into the Laughter Lounge of Loss, where grieving hearts find solace in unexpected smiles and where laughter becomes an integral part of the healing process.

Get ready to chuckle, snicker, and maybe even belly laugh as we uncover the quirky, the absurd, and the downright hilarious facets of navigating the turbulent seas of grief. Together, let's embrace the healing power of humor on this journey to rediscovering joy amid the shadows of sorrow.

Part 1: Welcome to the Laughter Lounge of Loss

In the quiet corners of sorrow, where tears stain the pages of our personal narratives, there exists a peculiar sanctum—a haven where laughter and grief share an intricate waltz. Welcome to the Laughter Lounge of Loss, an unconventional space where the echoes of mirth and the weight of loss coalesce in a dance that defies the conventional boundaries of mourning.

1. The Unexpected Harmony

Grief, often portrayed as a somber and solitary journey, reveals unexpected facets in the Laughter Lounge. Here, sorrow is not the antithesis of joy, but rather, a companion in an intricate choreography. It is a place where laughter becomes a salve for the soul, an unconventional melody that harmonizes with the discordant notes of loss.

2. A Comedy of Contradictions

In the midst of grief, laughter may seem a paradoxical intrusion —an unwelcome guest in a solemn gathering. However, within the Laughter Lounge, we come to understand that this interplay of emotions is not a contradiction but a nuanced expression of the human experience. Laughter, even in grief's embrace, is not a denial of pain but a testament to the complexity of our emotions.

3. An Invitation to Vulnerability

Entering the Laughter Lounge requires a willingness to embrace vulnerability. It beckons us to shed the armor of stoicism and allow ourselves the grace to find amusement amid anguish. Here, vulnerability is not a weakness but a strength, an acknowledgment that healing often begins in the tender spaces where laughter and tears converge.

4. Crafting a Narrative of Resilience

Within the Laughter Lounge, we embark on the journey of crafting a narrative of resilience. It is not a denial of the challenges that accompany loss but an intentional choice to navigate the terrain with humor as a compass. Laughter becomes a tool of empowerment, transforming adversity into an opportunity to redefine our relationship with grief.

5. The Grief-Stricken Stand-Up

Picture the Laughter Lounge as a stage where grief takes on the persona of a stand-up comedian. In this unconventional performance, the comedian, with tears in their eyes and a heavy heart, invites the audience to partake in the laughter that arises from the absurdity of life's tragicomedy. The punchlines are poignant, the humor is raw, and the audience—those who have known loss—nod in understanding.

6. Rediscovering Joy Amidst Sorrow

The Laughter Lounge is a haven for rediscovering joy amidst sorrow. It challenges us to seek moments of levity without guilt, acknowledging that the capacity for joy can coexist with the enduring ache of loss. Laughter, like a resilient blossom, finds its way through the cracks of grief, reminding us that joy need not be sacrificed at the altar of sorrow.

7. Shared Chuckles, Shared Comfort

In the Laughter Lounge, shared chuckles become shared comfort.

It is a communal space where individuals who have weathered the storm of grief come together to exchange stories, not only of loss but of the unexpected moments of hilarity that emerged in the midst of darkness. Laughter binds these narratives, weaving a tapestry of shared resilience.

As we step into the Laughter Lounge of Loss, let us embrace the paradoxes, honor the vulnerabilities, and allow ourselves the cathartic release of shared laughter. Together, we navigate the nuanced terrain of grief with a gentle understanding that within the echoes of mirth, we may find unexpected solace in the face of profound loss. Welcome to the Laughter Lounge, where tears and laughter dance in a rhythm known only to those who have braved the depths of grief's complex symphony.

Part 2: The Humorist's Toolkit

As we settle into the Laughter Lounge of Loss, it becomes apparent that navigating grief with humor requires a unique set of tools— a Humorist's Toolkit, if you will. These tools, forged in the fires of shared laughter and tears, are essential for those who seek not only solace but a genuine connection with the intricate dance of joy and sorrow.

1. The Chuckle Compass

The Chuckle Compass is the first tool in our Humorist's Toolkit. It is the internal guide that helps us navigate the uncharted territories of laughter within the landscape of loss. Like a compass pointing north, the Chuckle Compass directs us toward moments of levity, reminding us that even in the darkest hours, humor can be a guiding light.

2. The Mirthful Metaphor

In the Laughter Lounge, grief often wears the costume of a mirthful metaphor—a symbolic expression that transforms sorrow into an unexpected source of amusement. This tool allows us to view our experiences through a lens of whimsy, turning the seemingly mundane aspects of grief into opportunities for laughter.

3. The Satirical Sword

Grief's armor can be formidable, but armed with the Satirical Sword, we learn to pierce through its defenses with a touch of satire. This tool enables us to laugh at the absurdities of life, creating a space where the weight of grief is momentarily lifted by the pointed blade of humor. Satire becomes a shield against the solemn, allowing us to confront grief with a knowing smile.

4. The Irony Inkwell

In the Humorist's Toolkit, the Irony Inkwell is a vessel that holds the ink of irony, which we use to script moments of unexpected hilarity in the midst of grief. As we dip our quills into this inkwell, we find that irony becomes a powerful medium for storytelling—turning the tragic into the comic, and the comic into a poignant commentary on the human experience.

5. The Resilient Riddle Book

Grief often presents itself as an enigma, a riddle that lacks a clear solution. The Resilient Riddle Book in our toolkit helps us approach these mysteries with a sense of resilience. We learn to appreciate the absurdity of life's unanswered questions, finding solace in the laughter that arises from embracing the uncertainty of our grief-filled journey.

6. The Jester's Journal

Every humorist needs a place to chronicle their experiences, and in the Laughter Lounge, we have the Jester's Journal. This tool allows us to record the anecdotes, jokes, and whimsical observations that emerge from our encounters with grief. The act of journaling becomes a cathartic release, transforming the pages into a personal script where grief and laughter coalesce.

7. The Joyful Jigsaw

Grief is a complex puzzle, and the Joyful Jigsaw is our tool for assembling the scattered pieces into a mosaic of laughter. This tool encourages us to find joy in the unexpected connections between moments of sorrow. Like a jigsaw puzzle coming together, the Joyful Jigsaw allows us to discover the beauty that emerges when laughter and grief interlock.

8. The Compassionate Clown Nose

Perhaps the most important tool in our Humorist's Toolkit is the Compassionate Clown Nose. This whimsical accessory serves as a reminder that humor in the face of loss is not about masking pain but embracing it with compassion. Wearing the Compassionate Clown Nose, we acknowledge the depth of our sorrow while allowing laughter to coexist in the same heartfelt space.

As we explore the Laughter Lounge of Loss armed with these tools, let us remember that humor is not a diversion from grief but a companion on the journey. In the dance of joy and sorrow, these tools help us navigate the intricate steps, transforming grief into a poignant comedy where laughter and tears share the stage.

Chapter 2: "Foolish Frolics: 5 Stupid Things to Turn Tears into Giggles"

In Ana's pursuit of laughter amidst tears, she stumbled upon a treasure trove of hilariously absurd antics. This chapter, titled "Foolish Frolics," became a compendium of 5 Stupid Things designed to transform the somber symphony of sorrow into a whimsical medley of chuckles.

1. The Mirror Mime Show

Ana's first suggestion was the Mirror Mime Show—an exhibition of exaggerated facial expressions and silly gestures. In moments of melancholy, Ana would stand in front of the mirror, contorting her face into comical grimaces and adopting the antics of a melodramatic mime. The sheer absurdity of the Mirror Mime Show never failed to coax laughter from even the most stubborn tears.

2. The Dance of the Absurd

Next on the list was "The Dance of the Absurd." Ana proposed crafting an utterly ridiculous dance routine, complete with awkward moves and outlandish costumes. In times of sadness, she would put on a performance that could rival any avant-garde masterpiece. The ludicrous nature of the dance injected an element of joyful absurdity into the gloomiest of moments.

3. Singing the Alphabet Backward – with a Twist

Ana's third suggestion was to tackle the Alphabet Song but with a twist—singing it backward. This linguistic gymnastics not only distracted from the weight of sorrow but also provided a source of amusement as Ana navigated the alphabet in reverse, occasionally stumbling into unintentional hilarity.

4. The Unruly Hair Salon

For the fourth foolproof method, Ana recommended transforming moments of sadness into a visit to the imaginary "Unruly Hair Salon." Armed with an imaginary pair of scissors and a quirky hairdresser persona, Ana would playfully style her hair into outrageous configurations. The sheer absurdity of the Unruly Hair Salon antics never failed to break the chains of sorrow.

5. The Peculiar Pet Parade

The chapter's grand finale was "The Peculiar Pet Parade." Ana suggested enlisting imaginary pets, each with its own eccentric personality, and orchestrating a whimsical parade. Whether it was the invisible elephant doing the cha-cha or the silent parrot delivering punchlines, the Peculiar Pet Parade became a delightful carnival of laughter.

As Ana reveled in these 5 Stupid Things, she discovered that sometimes, the silliest and most absurd endeavors held the power to banish tears and usher in waves of laughter. Boa viagem through the foolish frolics, where Ana, armed with her arsenal of absurdity, transformed sorrow into a spectacle of joy.

Chapter 3: Complaints to the Cosmos: Hilarious Venting Sessions with a Deceased Husband

In the cosmic comedy of grief, Ana discovered a peculiar coping mechanism – engaging in comical complaint sessions with her departed husband, Jim. This unorthodox approach to venting became the inspiration for a chapter in her laughter-filled journey titled "Complaints to the Cosmos."

Part 1: The Imaginary Inbox of Interstellar Inquiries

Ana's cosmic complaint sessions often started with her addressing a makeshift "Imaginary Inbox of Interstellar Inquiries." Armed with a notepad and a flair for theatrical monologues, she would air her grievances to the cosmos, blaming Jim for everything from misplaced keys to the mysterious disappearance of socks in the laundry. The imaginary interstellar inbox, in Ana's mind, overflowed with cosmic chuckles.

Part 2: The Celestial Culinary Critique

One of Ana's favorite segments in the complaint sessions was the "Celestial Culinary Critique." While preparing meals, she would engage in animated discussions with Jim about his supposed interference in the kitchen. Accusing him of orchestrating culinary chaos from the afterlife, Ana turned mundane kitchen mishaps into a gastronomic comedy, with Jim being the mischievous maestro of mayhem.

Part 3: The Poltergeist Pranks Parody

The third act in Ana's cosmic comedy involved recounting "Poltergeist Pranks." Any minor inconvenience, from a misplaced book to flickering lights, became a potential poltergeist prank orchestrated by Jim. Ana's playful banter with the mischievous spirit of her departed husband turned these everyday occurrences into a series of lighthearted spectacles.

Part 4: Heavenly Household Hijinks

Ana's laughter-filled complaints extended to the realm of "Heavenly Household Hijinks." From imaginary dance parties in the living room to blaming Jim for the occasional mysteriously rearranged furniture, Ana turned the ordinary into the extraordinary in her celestial sitcom. The household hijinks, as per Ana's narrative, were orchestrated by a whimsical, otherworldly director – her late husband, Jim.

As Ana navigated the cosmic comedy of complaints, she discovered that even in the afterlife, Jim could be her partner in laughter. The venting sessions, filled with theatrics and absurd accusations, became a therapeutic avenue where grief and joy coexisted in a celestial dance. Boa viagem through the comical cosmos, where Ana, with her cosmic complaints, turned the echoes of loss into a symphony of laughter.

Chapter 4: "Conversations with Thin Air: Ana's Hilarious Heart-to-Heart with the Departed

In the whimsical world of grief, Ana stumbled upon a peculiar pastime – engaging in comical conversations with her deceased husband, Jim. This chapter, titled "Conversations with Thin Air," chronicled Ana's venture into the realm of talking to thin air and the ensuing laughter that echoed through the corridors of her solitude.

Part 1: The Invisible Interviewer

Ana's conversations often took the form of imaginary interviews where she played both the interviewer and interviewee. Armed with a pretend microphone, she'd ask Jim probing questions about the cosmic wonders beyond and the practicalities of afterlife logistics. The invisible interviewer, in Ana's mind, became a comedic character with a penchant for interstellar inquiries.

Part 2: The Quirky Quizmaster

Ana's dialogues transformed into a quirky quiz show, with Jim as the unsuspecting quizmaster. She'd fire off eccentric questions about the hypothetical hijinks in the afterlife – from celestial dance-offs to intergalactic cooking competitions. The imaginary quiz show turned grief into a game, with Ana embracing the role of a joyful contestant in the comedy of cosmic queries.

Part 3: The Solo Stand-Up Routine

In moments of solitude, Ana unleashed her inner stand-up comedian, performing a solo routine for her unseen audience – a whimsical audience comprised of thin air and the spirit of her late husband. The stand-up routine became a laughter-filled therapy session where Ana's comedic monologues transformed the echoes of grief into a symphony of chuckles.

Part 4: The Unfiltered Unburdening

The chapter reached its crescendo with Ana's unfiltered unburdening sessions. In candid, one-sided conversations, she'd express her joys, frustrations, and absurdities to the invisible presence of Jim. The seemingly crazy dialogues, spoken to thin air, became an unorthodox form of self-expression that allowed Ana to release the weight of grief with a generous dose of humor.

As Ana's laughter echoed through the walls, she discovered that talking to thin air wasn't a sign of insanity but a whimsical way of keeping the spirit of Jim alive in her heart. Boa viagem through the hilarious heart-to-heart conversations, where Ana, with her one-sided banter, turned solitude into a comedy club and thin air into an audience that applauded the laughter that emerged from the depths of loss.

Chapter 5 : Samba and Scones - Jim's Cultural Odyssey in Brazil

Part 1: The Samba Serendipity

British Jim, the epitome of reserved British charm, found himself in the midst of Brazil's pulsating culture, where samba beats and vibrant colors define the rhythm of life. Invited to a spontaneous samba street party in Rio de Janeiro, Jim, clad in his traditional suit, embarked on an unforgettable dance with the rhythm of Brazilian joy.

As the drumbeats echoed through the crowded streets, Jim's attempts to mimic the spirited samba dancers drew amused glances and hearty laughter from the locals. Undeterred, he embraced the carefree spirit of the celebration, twirling and swaying to the infectious music. Jim's samba serendipity became a symbol of cultural fusion, where British propriety met the lively soul of Brazilian carnival, creating a dance of laughter that transcended borders.

Part 2: Beachside Tea Extravaganza

Jim, determined to share a taste of British culture, organized a beachside tea extravaganza on the iconic Copacabana beach. Armed with teacups, a selection of teas, and an assortment of scones, he set up a charming tea party amidst the sun-kissed sands and the rhythmic sound of crashing waves.

Locals, initially puzzled by this peculiar beachside tea ceremony, soon joined in the festivities. Jim's meticulous pouring of tea, accompanied by proper etiquette, became a source of amusement. A sudden gust of wind sent sand flying, prompting laughter and applause from the impromptu gathering. The beachside tea extravaganza became a delightful spectacle that bridged cultural gaps and turned a traditional British ritual into a sun-soaked, sandy affair.

Part 3: Soccer, Scones, and a Symphony of Laughter

Jim's cultural odyssey in Brazil reached its pinnacle when he attended a local soccer match, a cornerstone of Brazilian passion. Dressed in his suit, Jim navigated the enthusiastic crowd with a basket of freshly baked scones in hand. As the stadium roared with cheers, Jim, undeterred by the fervor, offered scones to fellow spectators.

The juxtaposition of British tea-time traditions with the energetic atmosphere of a soccer match elicited a symphony of laughter from the crowd. Jim, initially seen as an anomaly, soon became a beloved figure, symbolizing the harmonious blend of diverse cultures. The soccer stadium, adorned with cheers and the aroma of scones, echoed with the universal language of joy.

In the end, Jim's immersion into Brazilian culture became a

testament to the power of laughter in forging connections across cultural boundaries. Through samba, beachside tea parties, and soccer matches, Jim discovered that the language of joy transcends nationality, creating a harmonious melody where British refinement dances alongside Brazilian exuberance.

Chapter 6: Tea, Tan, and Tango – A Comedy of Cultural Contrasts

Part 1: Tea, Tango, and Tropics

Enter British Jim, a paragon of English sensibilities, as he finds himself entangled in the tropical tapestry of Brazilian culture. His journey begins with an attempt to enjoy a traditional cup of tea in the bustling heart of São Paulo. Unbeknownst to Jim, the tropical climate had other plans.

As he delicately poured his tea on a charming outdoor terrace, a mischievous monkey, native to the region, swung down and snatched his scone. Jim's perfectly orchestrated tea time turned into a chaotic comedy of chasing the runaway pastry through the lively streets. The locals, amused by the spectacle, joined in the chase, turning Jim's pursuit of a peaceful tea into a tropical tango.

Part 2: Weather Whims and Witty Banter

Jim's exploration of Brazilian culture continued, this time with a visit to the beach. Armed with a meticulous plan for sunbathing in the English way, complete with SPF 50 and a wide-brimmed hat, Jim strolled onto Copacabana beach with unwavering determination.

However, the tropical sun had its own agenda. In no time, Jim transformed from a poised Englishman into a walking sunscreen advertisement, layered in a comical combination of creams and lotions. His attempt to maintain a stiff upper lip amid the sweltering heat became a humorous exchange of banter with beachgoers, who generously offered coconut water to the charmingly befuddled Brit.

Part 3: Soccer, Scones, and Spontaneity

Jim's encounter with Brazilian passion for soccer took an unexpected turn. Attending a local match, Jim brought along a basket of freshly baked scones, intending to share his love for British traditions. Little did he know, the fervor of Brazilian soccer fans would add a spicy twist to his afternoon tea.

As the crowd erupted into cheers, Jim, bewildered but undeterred, initiated a tea-time interlude during halftime. The fans, initially puzzled, soon joined in the laughter, creating a moment of cultural fusion where British scones met Brazilian soccer chants. The soccer stadium became a playground for unexpected camaraderie and lighthearted banter.

Part 4: Umbrellas, Umbrellas Everywhere

Jim's cultural comedy reached its zenith during a sudden downpour in Rio de Janeiro. Accustomed to the persistent drizzle of English rain, Jim confidently wielded his classic British umbrella, unfazed by the tropical tempest that awaited him.
To his surprise, the locals, accustomed to the spontaneous rain showers, opted for a more carefree approach. Jim's well-intentioned umbrella became a source of amusement as he navigated the crowded streets, unintentionally causing a sea of colorful umbrellas to dance around him. The once-stoic

Englishman found himself in the midst of a tropical storm turned into a lively tango of umbrellas and laughter.

In the end, Jim's cultural escapades in Brazil became a delightful symphony of laughter, where the contrasts between English reserve and Brazilian spontaneity transformed into a harmonious blend of traditions. Through tea, tan, and tango, Jim learned that sometimes the best way to navigate cultural differences is with a hearty dose of humor and a willingness to dance to the rhythm of the unexpected.

Chapter 7 Samba Flavors - Navigating the Gastronomic Carnival of Brazil

Brazil, a land of vibrant culture and pulsating rhythms, extends its carnival spirit to the realm of cuisine. As our adventurous protagonist, let's follow Jim on a gastronomic odyssey through the crazy and delectable world of Brazilian food.

Part 1: Feijoada Frolics

Jim's culinary escapade begins with a classic Brazilian dish, feijoada. Eager to embrace local customs, he joins a lively feast where the air is filled with the rich aroma of black beans, pork, and sausage. As Jim takes his first bite, the flavorful explosion sends him into a feijoada frolic, where the hearty flavors and lively music intertwine.

The locals, amused by Jim's enthusiastic feasting, encourage him to pair the dish with a caipirinha, Brazil's iconic cocktail. Jim's attempt at sipping the potent drink turns into a spontaneous samba as he finds himself swaying to the rhythm of both music and flavors.

Part 2: Coxinha Chronicles

Jim's journey through Brazilian cuisine ventures into coxinha territory, a beloved snack that captures the heart of locals. As he bites into the golden, deep-fried dough filled with shredded chicken, Jim is greeted by an explosion of flavors that takes him by surprise.

The locals, noticing Jim's delighted expression, playfully challenge him to a coxinha-eating contest. Jim, with his British politeness, accepts the challenge and discovers a newfound appreciation for this savory delight. The coxinha chronicles become a testament to the delightful chaos that unfolds when traditional Brazilian snacks meet Jim's refined taste buds.

Part 3: Açaí Antics

Jim, still savoring the memories of coxinha, ventures into the world of açaí, Brazil's superfood sensation. The vibrant purple bowls adorned with an array of toppings leave Jim both intrigued and slightly perplexed. Is it a dessert? Is it a meal? The answer lies in the delightful açaí antics that unfold.

Attempting to master the art of eating açaí with finesse, Jim soon finds himself adorned with purple splatters, turning the experience into an unintentional food art display. The locals, far from judging, join in the laughter, recognizing that açaí is not just a dish but an interactive performance.

Part 4: Brigadeiro Bliss

Jim's culinary carnival concludes with brigadeiro, the sweet treat that embodies the essence of Brazilian celebrations. The rich, chocolatey confections become Jim's guilty pleasure as he indulges in the brigadeiro bliss.

In an unexpected turn of events, Jim is invited to join a brigadeiro-making competition. His meticulous British approach clashes hilariously with the carefree, swirling motions of the locals. The brigadeiro bliss becomes a testament to the universal joy found in sharing sweet moments, regardless of cultural nuances.

In the end, Jim's journey through the crazy Brazilian food scene becomes a flavorful narrative of laughter, unexpected combinations, and a dance of tastes that transcends cultural boundaries. From feijoada frolics to açaí antics, every bite in Brazil tells a story, leaving Jim with a palate enriched by the delightful symphony of Samba flavors.

Chapter 8 : Lost and Found - Jim and Ana's Unexpected Journey in Favela da Rocinha

Part 1: The Curious Wanderers

Jim and Ana set out on a day of exploration within Favela da Rocinha, the vibrant and labyrinthine community that unfolded against the backdrop of Rio de Janeiro. Eager to uncover hidden gems, they meandered through narrow alleys, embraced by the lively atmosphere of the favela.

As they ventured deeper into Rocinha, captivated by the vibrant murals and the rhythmic beats of distant samba, Jim and Ana became engrossed in the vibrant tapestry of community life. Unbeknownst to them, the intricate maze of alleys began to blur the line between planned exploration and spontaneous adventure.

Part 2: The Alleyway Enigma

Lost in the winding alleys, Jim and Ana found themselves immersed in a captivating blend of colors, sounds, and the resilient spirit of Rocinha. The initial excitement of discovery soon gave way to a realization—they were navigating an alleyway enigma, where each turn seemed to present a new and unfamiliar scene.

Undeterred by the unexpected twists and turns, Jim and Ana embraced the unpredictability of their journey. The locals, noticing their confusion, offered friendly gestures and directions in a blend of Portuguese and smiles, creating a sense of camaraderie amid the confusion.

Part 3: Unexpected Connections

As Jim and Ana navigated the favela's maze, they stumbled upon a communal gathering where locals were sharing stories, laughter, and a traditional meal. The warmth of the community embraced them, turning their unintentional detour into an opportunity to connect with Rocinha's heart.

Despite the language barrier, Jim and Ana found themselves engaged in conversations, sharing laughter, and experiencing the genuine hospitality of the residents. The initial sense of being lost transformed into a feeling of being unexpectedly found—in the midst of Rocinha's rich culture and the kindness of its people.

Part 4: Sunset Over Serendipity

As the sun began its descent, casting a warm glow over Rocinha, Jim and Ana reached an overlook that offered a panoramic view of the favela and the city beyond. The sun's rays painted the buildings in hues of gold, revealing the beauty that had been hidden in the intricate alleys.

In that serendipitous moment, overlooking the favela they had initially gotten lost in, Jim and Ana reflected on the day's unexpected journey. Their adventure became a tale of resilience, community, and the transformative power of embracing the unknown. Lost in Rocinha, they had found not only the way back but a deeper connection to a vibrant community that defied stereotypes and welcomed them with open arms.

In the end, Jim and Ana's day of getting lost in Favela da Rocinha became a chapter of unexpected beauty—a story of serendipity, cultural exploration, and the profound moments that arise when wanderers embrace the uncharted paths.

Chapter 9: "Samba, Sweat, and Swear Words"

In the lively streets of Rio de Janeiro, our unsuspecting language learner, Jim, finds himself thrust into a whirlwind of samba beats and Portuguese pitfalls. His language adventure begins with the rhythmic pulse of the city, accompanied by the toe-tapping melodies of street musicians.

As Jim attempts to master the basics of Brazilian Portuguese, he quickly realizes that language learning comes with its fair share of challenges – both linguistic and physical. The vibrant dance culture of Brazil becomes Jim's unexpected classroom, where he discovers that mastering samba steps is just as crucial as conjugating verbs.

In a comical series of missteps, Jim attempts to dance his way through conversations, inadvertently using the wrong words and earning puzzled looks from locals. As he sweats through samba classes, he also learns that the Portuguese language has its fair share of tricky sounds and tongue twisters.

But it's not all fun and games. Jim soon discovers that navigating the colorful streets of Brazil requires more than just dance moves – it demands a robust vocabulary, including a few choice swear words. In a humorous encounter with a passionate street vendor, Jim inadvertently uses a slang term that leaves the vendor in stitches and earns him a few friendly slaps on the back.

"Samba, Sweat, and Swear Words" sets the stage for Jim's comedic journey into Brazilian Portuguese, highlighting the unexpected

blend of rhythm, language, and cultural nuances that make learning this vibrant language an unforgettable adventure. As Jim stumbles and shimmies his way through the streets of Rio, readers can't help but join him in the laughter,
realizing that sometimes, the best language lessons come with a beat.

Part 1: The Rhythm of Portuguese

As the sun dipped below the horizon, casting a warm glow over the vibrant streets of Rio de Janeiro, our language enthusiasts gathered in the spirited classrooms of Portu-giggles. The air buzzed with anticipation, and the rhythmic beats of samba set the tone for their linguistic adventure.

The teacher, a lively Brazilian language maestro, greeted the eager learners with a samba-infused "Bom dia!" Laughter echoed through the room as the class embarked on the lively dance of Brazilian Portuguese. Vowels and consonants became partners in a linguistic tango, and the students found themselves caught up in the infectious rhythm of the language.

"Repeat after me," the teacher exclaimed, setting the pace for a linguistic samba. With every pronunciation, the room transformed into a linguistic Carnaval, and the learners, despite initial stumbling, soon discovered the joy of dancing to the unique beat of Portuguese.

In this rhythm-infused atmosphere, language barriers melted away, and the classroom became a stage where the samba of Brazilian Portuguese unfolded. Laughter, like a percussive instrument, punctuated the lessons, turning language learning into a joyful celebration of sounds and rhythms.

As our intrepid language enthusiasts navigated the first steps of their linguistic samba, the realization dawned that Brazilian Portuguese wasn't merely a language; it was a lively dance that they were learning to perform with the grace and flair of a seasoned dancer. The rhythm of Portuguese, set against the backdrop of laughter, became the heartbeat of their Portu-giggles adventure.

Part 2: The Sweat of Conjugations

The next chapter of the Portu-giggles adventure unfolded as our language enthusiasts dove headfirst into the linguistic gymnasium of verb conjugations. The classroom, now a metaphorical fitness center, echoed with the rhythmic beats of conjugation drills.

The teacher, armed with a linguistic whistle, led the class through the rigorous workout routine of Portuguese verbs. "Eu falo, tu falas, ele fala," the rhythmic chanting began. Sweat beads formed on foreheads as the students navigated the intricate steps of conjugating verbs, akin to a linguistic Zumba session.

Laughter intertwined with the linguistic exertion, turning the seemingly mundane task of verb conjugations into a comedic spectacle. The teacher, with a twinkle in their eye, encouraged the learners to embrace the sweat, assuring them that each drop represented a step closer to mastering the dance of Portuguese grammar.

As conjugations became more complex, the camaraderie among the language enthusiasts grew. Encouraging words and shared laughter created an atmosphere where the sweat of conjugations wasn't just a sign of effort but a badge of honor—a testament to their commitment to mastering the linguistic dance floor.

In the end, as the linguistic fitness class concluded, our learners wiped their brows, not just from the sweat of conjugations, but from the exhilaration of realizing the strength in their linguistic muscles. The classroom, now a linguistic gymnasium, transformed into a place where the sweat of effort and the joy of progress coexisted in perfect harmony. And so, with a triumphant cheer, the Portu-gigglers emerged, sweat and all, ready for the next linguistic dance challenge.

Part 3: The Art of Swear Words

With the echoes of samba beats still reverberating through the linguistic gymnasium, our intrepid language enthusiasts gathered for the third act of their Portu-giggles adventure—the artful exploration of Brazilian colloquialisms and, yes, a lesson in the strategic use of swear words.

The teacher, with a mischievous glint in their eye, announced, "Today, we dive into the colorful expressions that add a spicy flair to Brazilian Portuguese." Laughter erupted, a precursor to the linguistic rollercoaster they were about to embark upon.

The classroom atmosphere shifted as the teacher shared common colloquialisms, offering insights into the nuanced meanings and cultural contexts behind each phrase. The learners, now language connoisseurs-in-the-making, navigated the delicate balance between cultural sensitivity and linguistic curiosity.

As the lesson ventured into the realm of swear words, the room transformed into a theater of linguistic audacity. Chuckles mingled with exclamations as the students practiced the artful delivery of these expressions. The teacher, acting as a linguistic maestro, guided them through the nuanced tones and inflections that turned a simple word into a comedic masterpiece.

The classroom, now a sanctuary of linguistic irreverence, became a space where laughter thrived amidst the exploration of colloquial nuances. The students, armed with newfound linguistic weaponry, found themselves not only learning a language but also immersing in the rich tapestry of Brazilian expressions.

In the end, as the class concluded, the learners emerged with a twinkle in their eyes and a linguistic toolkit that extended beyond the conventional. The art of swear words, approached with a sense of humor, became an unexpected highlight of their Portu-giggles journey—a chapter where laughter and learning walked hand in hand through the vibrant streets of Brazilian Portuguese.

Chapter 10

As our intrepid language learner, Jim, continues his escapades in Brazil, he stumbles upon an age-old tradition that promises both linguistic enlightenment and a good time: the Great Caipirinha Challenge. Little does Jim know that this cocktail-fueled adventure is about to shake up his understanding of Portuguese pronouns.

The chapter opens with Jim finding himself in a lively bar, surrounded by locals clinking glasses and laughing uproariously. Eager to immerse himself in the culture, he decides to try the iconic Brazilian cocktail, the caipirinha. However, Jim soon realizes that ordering this deceptively simple drink is a linguistic hurdle in itself.

As he attempts to communicate his drink order, Jim discovers the intricate dance of Portuguese pronouns. The subtle nuances between "tu" and "você" leave him tongue-tied, and the bartender, with a mischievous twinkle in her eye, playfully corrects his grammar. Jim's quest for the perfect caipirinha becomes an unintentional lesson in the importance of pronouns in Brazilian Portuguese.

The Great Caipirinha Challenge takes an unexpected turn when Jim, determined to impress the locals, decides to mix his own drink. Armed with a recipe and a questionable understanding of the language, he embarks on a comedic journey through the world of cocktail-making, inadvertently turning the bar into his makeshift language laboratory.

As Jim fumbles with limes, sugar, and a generous pour of

cachaça, he unwittingly incorporates Portuguese pronouns into his cocktail shenanigans. The bar patrons, amused by his efforts, join in the linguistic revelry, offering tips and corrections between sips of caipirinha.

"The Great Caipirinha Challenge: Mixing Drinks and Pronouns" serves up a delightful blend of humor and language learning, leaving Jim – and readers – with a newfound appreciation for the importance of pronouns and a memorable recipe for a caipirinha, with a side of Portuguese wisdom.

Part 1: The Great Caipirinha Challenge: Mixing Drinks and Pronouns

As the sun dipped low over the horizon, casting a warm glow over the Portu-giggles language school, our enthusiastic learners gathered for a new chapter in their Brazilian Portuguese adventure—the Great Caipirinha Challenge. The classroom buzzed with anticipation, and the air was thick with the promise of both linguistic exploration and a touch of mixology.

The teacher, doubling as a master mixologist for this occasion, stood at the front of the class, holding a shaker and a selection of tropical fruits. "Today, my friends, we embark on a journey where pronouns and cocktails collide in a delightful symphony of flavor and language," they proclaimed, eliciting a ripple of excitement among the learners.

The Language Libations Begin

The lesson commenced with a linguistic twist—pronouns. Each learner received a personalized pronoun that would be their linguistic companion for the day. Laughter echoed through the room as students embraced their newfound linguistic identities, setting the stage for a uniquely immersive experience.

As the teacher guided them through the intricacies of Portuguese pronouns, the class discovered the rhythmic dance between words, much like the samba beats they had previously encountered. Pronouns, it seemed, were the linguistic partners in the dance of conversation, providing a fluidity that mirrored the steps of a well-practiced dance routine.

Into the Cocktail Cauldron

With pronouns firmly in grasp, the classroom transformed into a lively caipirinha workshop. The teacher, now wearing a mixologist hat, demonstrated the art of crafting the perfect Brazilian cocktail. Fruits were sliced, limes were squeezed, and the unmistakable aroma of fresh mint filled the air.

As the learners approached the makeshift cocktail bar, they realized that the challenge wasn't just about mixing drinks but also about mastering the art of conversation with their personalized pronouns. Laughter bubbled alongside the caipirinhas as the class navigated both the literal and figurative blending of language and libations.

In this fusion of linguistic and mixological exploration, the Great Caipirinha Challenge became more than just a lesson—it became a celebration of the vivacious spirit of Brazilian Portuguese, where language and leisure danced hand in hand. The classroom, now a lively cocktail lounge, set the stage for a chapter where sips of caipirinhas were accompanied by the intoxicating joy of linguistic discovery.

Chapter 11: "Surviving the Linguistic Jungle: 20 Essential Portuguese Phrases for the Adventurous Traveler"

In this practical chapter, Jim equips himself with a survival kit of essential Portuguese phrases, transforming his journey through Brazil into a seamless and enjoyable adventure.

1. **Olá (Hello):** Jim kicks off his survival list with the universal greeting, ensuring he can warmly connect with locals wherever he goes.

2. **Por favor (Please):** Recognizing the importance of politeness, Jim adds this phrase to his arsenal, making interactions smoother and more pleasant.

3. **Obrigado/Obrigada (Thank you - Male/Female):** Jim quickly learns the significance of expressing gratitude, mastering this phrase to convey appreciation during his travels.

4. **Desculpe (Excuse me/I'm sorry):** Understanding that politeness is key, Jim adds this phrase to navigate crowded markets and public spaces with grace.

5. **Com licença (Excuse me):** Jim ensures he can politely navigate through crowds and attract attention when needed.

6. **Quanto custa? (How much does it cost?):** Armed with this phrase, Jim confidently ventures into local markets, ready to haggle for the best prices.

7. **Onde fica o banheiro? (Where is the bathroom?):** Realizing the importance of knowing where facilities are, Jim ensures he can make a quick inquiry in any situation.

8. **Eu não entendo (I don't understand):** Jim acknowledges that language barriers might arise, making this phrase essential for seeking clarification.

9. **Fala inglês? (Do you speak English?):** In case of more complex conversations, Jim learns to ask for English speakers, bridging the communication gap.

10. **Pode repetir, por favor? (Can you repeat, please?):** Building on his quest for understanding, Jim adds this phrase to ensure clear communication in all situations.

11. **Estou perdido (I am lost):** Recognizing the possibility of getting lost in the vibrant streets, Jim prepares for this common scenario.

12. **Me ajude, por favor (Help me, please):** For those moments when Google Maps fails him, Jim ensures he can seek assistance from friendly locals.

13. **Gostaria de (I would like):** Ready to indulge in local cuisine, Jim learns this phrase to smoothly place orders at restaurants and eateries.

14. **Qual é o seu nome? (What is your name?):** Understanding the importance of forging connections, Jim adds this question to his conversational toolkit.

15. **Onde é a estação de trem/ônibus? (Where is the train/bus station?):** For seamless travel, Jim makes sure he can navigate public transportation with ease.

16. **Estou com fome (I am hungry):** Preparing for his culinary adventures, Jim ensures he can express his basic needs, starting with hunger.

17. **Estou com sede (I am thirsty):** Jim recognizes the importance of staying hydrated, particularly in the Brazilian heat.

18. **Estou aqui a turismo (I am here for tourism):** Jim wants to ensure locals understand his purpose, fostering positive interactions.

19. **Pode tirar uma foto, por favor? (Can you take a photo, please?):** Ever the tourist, Jim adds this phrase to his repertoire, ensuring he can capture memories with the locals' help.

20. **Tenha um bom dia (Have a good day):** Jim wraps up his survival kit with a friendly farewell, leaving a positive impression wherever he goes.

Armed with these 20 essential Portuguese phrases, Jim transforms his journey into a linguistic adventure, navigating the vibrant streets of Brazil with confidence, courtesy, and a good dose of cultural appreciation.

Chapter 12 : "Talking Like a Local: 50 Brazilian Portuguese Expressions and Slangs to Spice Up Your Conversations"

In this chapter, Jim dives headfirst into the colorful world of Brazilian Portuguese expressions and slangs, eager to add a touch of authenticity to his conversations and truly connect with the locals.

1. **Legal (Cool/Good):** Jim quickly learns that in Brazil, everything that's cool or good is simply "legal."

2. **Beleza (Beauty):** Brazilians use this expression to mean "okay" or "got it." Jim adopts it as a versatile addition to his vocabulary.

3. **Valeu (Thanks):** A casual way to say thank you, Jim realizes that "valeu" is the go-to expression for showing gratitude.

4. **Muito show (Very cool):** To emphasize just how awesome something is, Jim incorporates this expression into his daily conversations.

5. **Cara (Dude/Guy):** Jim discovers that "cara" is the Brazilian equivalent of "dude" and starts using it to address his new friends.

6. **Puxar a brasa para a sardinha (To pull the coals to one's sardine):** This amusing expression means advocating for oneself or promoting one's interests. Jim finds it quite entertaining.

7. **Deixa pra lá (Let it go):** Embracing the laid-back Brazilian

attitude, Jim starts using this expression to brush off minor issues.

8. **Pô (Well):** A versatile interjection, Jim adopts "pô" to express surprise, disbelief, or even mild frustration.

9. **Fica a dica (Here's the tip):** Jim discovers that this phrase is used when offering advice or sharing a helpful hint.

10. **Dar um jeito (To figure it out):** Understanding the importance of adaptability, Jim adds this expression to his arsenal for problem-solving.

11. **Agora é que são elas (Now things are going to get tricky):** Jim encounters this expression when faced with a challenging situation, realizing it means things are about to get complicated.

12. **Fazer as pazes (To make peace):** Learning the importance of reconciliation, Jim uses this phrase to mend relationships.

13. **Pagar mico (To pay a monkey):** Amused by the imagery, Jim discovers this expression means to embarrass oneself in public.

14. **Deu ruim (It went wrong):** When things don't go as planned, Jim now uses this slang to express his frustration.

15. **Rachar a conta (To split the bill):** Jim embraces the Brazilian way of dividing expenses, using this phrase when dining out with friends.

16. **Estar com a corda toda (To be with the rope all):** Jim chuckles at this expression, realizing it means someone is full of energy and ready to party.

17. **Dormir de conchinha (To sleep in the little shell):** Jim blushes as he learns this cute expression for cuddling while sleeping.

18. **Está com a macaca (To be with the monkey):** Jim discovers this amusing way of saying someone is in a bad mood or acting strange.

19. **Matar a cobra e mostrar o pau (To kill the snake and show the stick):** Jim raises an eyebrow at this expression, realizing it means to accomplish something difficult and prove it.

20. **Fazer a fila andar (To make the line move):** Jim learns this phrase as a way of saying someone is moving on after a breakup.

21. **Queima filme (Burns film):** Jim chuckles at this slang for an embarrassing situation that ruins one's reputation.

22. **Encher linguiça (To fill the sausage):** Jim finds the humor in this expression, understanding it means to talk excessively without getting to the point.

23. **Pão-duro (Hard bread):** Jim discovers this slang for a stingy or miserly person and adopts it for playful banter.

24. **Bicho grilo (Cricket bug):** Jim encounters this term for a person with alternative or hippie tendencies and adds it to his list of amusing expressions.

25. **Fazer uma vaquinha (To make a little cow):** Jim realizes this phrase means to collect money from a group for a shared expense.

26. **Meter a colher (To put in the spoon):** Jim laughs at this slang, understanding it means to interfere in someone else's business.

27. **Estar a fim (To be in the mood):** Jim adds this phrase to his vocabulary when expressing interest in something or someone.

28. **Chutar o balde (To kick the bucket):** Jim discovers this expression for giving up or quitting when faced with challenges.

29. **Dar uma canja (To give a chicken broth):** Jim finds this phrase amusing, realizing it means to do something effortlessly or show off.

30. **Pé de chinelo (Sandal foot):** Jim chuckles at this term for someone of low social status or importance.

31. **Chover no molhado (To rain on the wet):** Jim learns this phrase for stating the obvious and starts using it to add a humorous touch to his observations.

32. **Olá (Hello):** Jim kicks off his survival list with the universal greeting, ensuring he can warmly connect with locals wherever he goes.

33. **Por favor (Please):** Recognizing the importance of politeness, Jim adds this phrase to his arsenal, making interactions smoother and more pleasant.

34. **Obrigado/Obrigada (Thank you - Male/Female):** Jim quickly learns the significance of expressing gratitude, mastering this phrase to convey appreciation during his travels.

35. **Desculpe (Excuse me/I'm sorry):** Understanding that politeness is key, Jim adds this phrase to navigate crowded markets and public spaces with grace.

36. **Com licença (Excuse me):** Jim ensures he can politely navigate through crowds and attract attention when needed.

37. **Quanto custa? (How much does it cost?):** Armed with this phrase, Jim confidently ventures into local markets, ready to haggle for the best prices.

38. **Onde fica o banheiro? (Where is the bathroom?):** Realizing the importance of knowing where facilities are, Jim ensures he can make a quick inquiry in any situation.

39. **Eu não entendo (I don't understand):** Jim acknowledges that language barriers might arise, making this phrase essential for seeking clarification.

40. **Fala inglês? (Do you speak English?):** In case of more complex conversations, Jim learns to ask for English speakers, bridging the communication gap.

41. **Pode repetir, por favor? (Can you repeat, please?):** Building on his quest for understanding, Jim adds this phrase to ensure clear communication in all situations.

42. **Estou perdido (I am lost):** Recognizing the possibility of getting lost in the vibrant streets, Jim prepares for this common scenario.

43. **Me ajude, por favor (Help me, please):** For those moments when Google Maps fails him, Jim ensures he can seek assistance from friendly locals.

44. **Gostaria de (I would like):** Ready to indulge in local cuisine, Jim learns this phrase to smoothly place orders at restaurants and eateries.

45. **Qual é o seu nome? (What is your name?):** Understanding the importance of forging connections, Jim adds this question to his conversational toolkit.

46. **Onde é a estação de trem/ônibus? (Where is the train/bus station?):** For seamless travel, Jim makes sure he can navigate public transportation with ease.

47. **Estou com fome (I am hungry):** Preparing for his culinary adventures, Jim ensures he can express his basic needs, starting with hunger.

48. **Estou com sede (I am thirsty):** Jim recognizes the importance of staying hydrated, particularly in the Brazilian heat.

49. **Estou aqui a turismo (I am here for tourism):** Jim wants to ensure locals understand his purpose, fostering positive interactions.

50. **Pode tirar uma foto, por favor? (Can you take a photo, please?):** Ever the tourist, Jim adds this phrase to his repertoire, ensuring he can capture memories with the locals' help.

51. **Tenha um bom dia (Have a good day):** Jim wraps up his

survival kit with a friendly farewell, leaving a positive impression wherever he goes.

Armed with these 50 essential Portuguese phrases, Jim transforms his journey into a linguistic adventure, navigating the vibrant streets of Brazil with confidence, courtesy, and a good dose of cultural appreciation.

Chapter 13: "Bizarre Beauties: Strange and Wonderful Sights on the Streets of Brazil"

As Jim takes leisurely strolls through the vibrant streets of Brazil, he can't help but marvel at the kaleidoscope of peculiar and delightful scenes that unfold before his eyes. This chapter chronicles Jim's encounters with the strange and wonderful, showcasing the unique charm that makes Brazil a captivating tapestry of eccentricities.

1. **Capoeira on the Sidewalks:** Jim is mesmerized as he stumbles upon impromptu capoeira performances right on the sidewalks. The rhythmic movements and acrobatics create a spectacle that blends seamlessly with the energy of the streets.

2. **Street Art Extravaganza:** Brazil's walls transform into canvases, and Jim finds himself surrounded by an explosion of vibrant street art. From breathtaking murals to quirky graffiti, every corner tells a visual story that adds an artistic flair to the urban landscape.

3. **Floating Fruit Markets:** Jim is taken aback when he sees boats transformed into floating markets on the Amazon River. Vendors skillfully navigate the waters, offering fresh fruits and local delicacies to passersby, creating a surreal shopping experience.

4. **Dressed-Up Utility Poles:** Brazil's creativity knows no bounds, and Jim can't help but smile at the utility poles dressed up as characters. From superheroes to animals, these quirky

installations bring a touch of whimsy to the streets.

5. **Parading Pets:** Jim witnesses a parade like no other when locals take their pets for a walk, decked out in vibrant costumes. Dogs, cats, and even birds strut their stuff, turning the streets into a lively pet fashion show.

6. **Beachside Soccer Matches:** A casual walk along the coastline turns into a front-row seat for impromptu beach soccer matches. Locals showcase their skills with the ocean waves as a backdrop, turning the sandy shores into a soccer enthusiast's dream.

7. **Dance-Offs in Public Squares:** Jim is drawn into the infectious rhythm of spontaneous dance-offs in public squares. Whether it's samba, forró, or a mix of styles, the squares become stages for joyful expressions of Brazilian dance culture.

8. **Colorful Umbrella-Lined Streets:** Jim is greeted by a kaleidoscope of colors as streets are adorned with hanging umbrellas. The vibrant umbrellas provide shade and create a whimsical ambiance that transforms the ordinary into the extraordinary.

9. **Mobile Fruit Vendors on Bicycles:** Jim is amused by the ingenuity of mobile fruit vendors pedaling through the streets on customized bicycles. Laden with an array of tropical fruits, these vendors bring the market directly to the neighborhoods.

10. **Public Fruit Trees:** Jim discovers a surprising sight as he encounters public fruit trees lining the streets. Locals freely pluck mangoes, guavas, and other fruits, creating a sense of communal abundance within the urban landscape.

11. **Synchronized Traffic Chaos:** Navigating the bustling streets, Jim witnesses a peculiar form of traffic coordination. Despite the apparent chaos, drivers and pedestrians seamlessly weave through the labyrinth, creating an orchestrated dance of movement.

12. **Floating Bookstore on the Amazon:** Jim is intrigued when he encounters a floating bookstore on the Amazon River. The unique shop offers a diverse collection of books, creating an unconventional literary experience amid the river's currents.

13. **Carnival Preparations in Unexpected Places:** Jim is amazed at the year-round preparations for Carnival. From costume workshops in alleys to spontaneous samba rehearsals in parks, the streets come alive with the anticipation of the grand celebration.

14. **Capivara Crossings:** In urban parks, Jim encounters capybaras casually crossing pathways. These giant rodents, native to Brazil, add a touch of the wild to the cityscape, creating unexpected encounters with the country's diverse wildlife.

15. **Mobile Coconut Water Vendors:** Jim delights in the convenience of mobile vendors pushing carts loaded with fresh coconuts. The sound of machetes skillfully opening coconuts becomes a melody on the streets, offering a refreshing respite to passersby.

16. **Giant Sand Sculptures on the Beach:** Jim is amazed by the intricate sand sculptures that emerge on Brazil's beaches. Talented artists create massive sculptures, ranging from mythical creatures to iconic landmarks, turning the coastline into an open-air art gallery.

17. **Sunset Drum Circles:** As the sun sets, Jim stumbles upon spontaneous drum circles on the beach. Locals and tourists alike join in, creating a rhythmic soundtrack that harmonizes with the colors of the setting sun.

18. **Street Food Innovations:** Jim's taste buds are tantalized by innovative street food offerings. From acarajé to tapioca pancakes, the streets become a culinary adventure, with vendors showcasing the diversity of Brazil's gastronomic delights.

19. **Hammock Street Siestas:** Jim observes the laid-back

lifestyle as locals string hammocks between trees, creating makeshift siesta spots in public spaces. The streets become a canvas for relaxation, with hammocks swaying gently in the breeze.

20. **Jewelry-Making on the Streets:** Jim is captivated by the skillful hands of street artisans crafting intricate jewelry on sidewalks. The streets transform into open-air workshops, where creativity flourishes, and passersby can witness the birth of unique handmade treasures.

In this chapter, Jim's walks through Brazil become a kaleidoscopic adventure, where every street corner reveals a delightful surprise. From the whimsical to the awe-inspiring, the streets of Brazil unfold as a testament to the country's vibrant culture and the art of embracing the extraordinary in the everyday.

Chapter 14: "Brazilian Marvels: 50 Unique Things Found Only in Brazil"

As Jim immerses himself in the rich tapestry of Brazilian culture and landscapes, he discovers an array of extraordinary phenomena and treasures that are exclusive to this diverse and vibrant country. This chapter unveils 50 remarkable aspects of Brazil that captivate Jim's imagination and contribute to the unique charm of this South American giant.

1. **Amazon Rainforest:** Brazil hosts the majority of the Amazon Rainforest, the largest tropical rainforest on Earth, home to an unparalleled biodiversity of flora and fauna.

2. **Cristo Redentor (Christ the Redeemer):** The iconic statue towering over Rio de Janeiro, offering breathtaking panoramic views of the city.

3. **Carnival:** Brazil's Carnival is a world-famous celebration, showcasing elaborate parades, vibrant costumes, and samba rhythms that define the country's festive spirit.

4. **Pantanal:** The world's largest tropical wetland area, the Pantanal is a haven for wildlife enthusiasts, offering a unique ecosystem teeming with diverse species.

5. **Guaraná Antarctica:** A popular Brazilian soft drink made from the guaraná fruit, known for its distinctive flavor and energizing properties.

6. **Ipanema Beach:** One of the most famous beaches in the world, known for its golden sands, lively atmosphere, and iconic

mosaic promenade.

7. **Açaí Berry:** Açaí bowls, made from the antioxidant-rich açaí berry, have become a global sensation, but Brazil remains the primary source of this superfood.

8. **Fernando de Noronha:** An archipelago with crystal-clear waters, white-sand beaches, and vibrant marine life, making it a coveted destination for nature lovers.

9. **Caipirinha:** Brazil's national cocktail, made with cachaça, sugar, and lime, representing the perfect blend of sweetness and citrusy freshness.

10. **Feijoada:** A hearty black bean stew with pork, sausage, and beef, showcasing the delicious flavors of Brazilian cuisine.

11. **Pão de Queijo:** These delectable cheese bread balls are a staple in Brazilian breakfasts, snacks, and celebrations.

12. **Futebol (Football):** Brazil's love for football is unrivaled, and the country has produced some of the greatest players and memorable moments in the sport's history.

13. **Samba:** The infectious rhythm of samba is the heartbeat of Brazilian music and dance, creating an indelible mark on the global cultural stage.

14. **Toucans:** These colorful and distinctive birds are native to Brazil, representing a vibrant symbol of the country's diverse wildlife.

15. **Rio Negro and Rio Solimões Confluence:** The Meeting of Waters, where the two rivers merge but do not immediately mix due to differences in temperature, speed, and water density.

16. **Brazilian Wax:** The concept of the Brazilian wax, popularized in Brazil, has become a global beauty trend for personal grooming.

17. **Sugarloaf Mountain:** A granite peak with breathtaking

views of Rio de Janeiro, accessible by cable car, offering a unique perspective of the city.

18. **Caipirinha Ice Cream:** A Brazilian twist on a classic treat, featuring the flavors of the iconic cocktail in frozen form.

19. **Jabuticaba Tree:** This unique tree bears fruit directly on its trunk, resembling grape-like clusters, providing a fascinating sight in Brazilian landscapes.

20. **Telenovelas:** Brazil's passion for telenovelas, or soap operas, has led to a thriving industry producing dramatic and entertaining television series.

21. **Brazil Nut Tree:** The Brazil nut tree, native to the Amazon Rainforest, produces large fruits containing the prized Brazil nuts.

22. **Tropical Fruit Varieties:** Brazil boasts an abundance of exotic fruits, including cupuaçu, guava, pitanga, and maracuja, adding a burst of tropical flavors to the culinary scene.

23. **Carnival Blocos:** These vibrant street parties and parades during Carnival bring communities together in a celebration of music, dance, and revelry.

24. **Tribal Festivals:** Indigenous festivals and celebrations, such as the Boi-Bumbá festival in the Amazon, showcase the rich cultural heritage of Brazil's native communities.

25. **Cachaça Distilleries:** Brazil is the birthplace of cachaça, the sugarcane spirit used in the production of the famous caipirinha cocktail.

26. **The Selarón Steps:** The Escadaria Selarón in Rio de Janeiro, adorned with colorful tiles from over 60 countries, creating a mesmerizing mosaic art installation.

27. **Avocado Ice Cream:** A creamy and delicious dessert popular in Brazil, showcasing the versatility of this beloved fruit.

28. **Brazilian Bikinis:** Known for their bold and colorful

designs, Brazilian bikinis have become synonymous with stylish beachwear worldwide.

29. **Belo Horizonte's Mercado Central:** A bustling market offering a sensory feast of spices, cheeses, meats, and traditional Brazilian delicacies.

30. **Bahia's Afro-Brazilian Culture:** The state of Bahia preserves a rich Afro-Brazilian heritage, expressed through music, dance, and religious traditions.

31. **Festa Junina:** Brazil's traditional June festivals, featuring lively dances, colorful costumes, and an array of delicious treats in celebration of São João (Saint John).

32. **Street Barbecues (Churrasco de Rua):** The enticing aroma of grilling meats fills the air as street vendors offer mouthwatering barbecue skewers to passersby.

33. **Carioca Funk:** A genre of electronic dance music originating in Rio de Janeiro, known for its energetic beats and vibrant dance culture.

34. **Cocada:** A sweet coconut dessert made with sugar, coconut, and other flavorings, reflecting Brazil's love for coconut-based treats.

35. **Brazilian Waxing Salons:** Brazil pioneered the widespread adoption of the Brazilian waxing technique for hair removal.

36. **Arara Parrots:** These colorful and charismatic parrots are native to Brazil, adding a lively touch to the country's diverse birdlife.

37. **Amazon River Dolphins:** Pink and gray river dolphins, also known as botos, inhabit the Amazon River, captivating observers with their unique appearance and behavior.

38. **Manguebeat Music:** Originating in Recife, Manguebeat is a fusion of traditional Brazilian music with rock, hip hop, and other

contemporary styles.

39. **Canga Beachwear:** Colorful and versatile, the canga is a multipurpose piece of fabric used as beachwear, creating a distinctive Brazilian beach culture.

40. **Tropical Forest Fruits in Ice Cream:** Street vendors offer an array of tropical fruit ice creams, including cupua

Important Note:

Coxinha and Caipirinha, why do you have to try?

Embarking on a culinary journey through Brazil, one simply cannot afford to miss the delightful duo of Coxinha and Caipirinha, a dynamic duo that encapsulates the essence of Brazilian flavors. Coxinha, a savory snack with a crispy exterior and a delectably seasoned shredded chicken filling, is a bite-sized burst of Brazilian comfort food. Its golden-brown exterior gives way to a moist and flavorful interior, making it a culinary masterpiece that locals hold dear to their hearts. Paired seamlessly with the iconic Caipirinha, a cocktail made with Brazil's sugarcane spirit, cachaça, lime, and sugar, the combination is a harmonious dance of savory and refreshing notes. The crispness of the Coxinha complements the zesty sweetness of the Caipirinha, creating a culinary symphony that embodies the vibrancy and diversity of Brazilian gastronomy. To savor Coxinha and Caipirinha is to immerse oneself in the soulful rhythm of Brazilian cuisine, where every bite and sip tells a tale of rich flavors and cultural celebration. It's a culinary experience that beckons adventurers to indulge in the irresistible allure of Brazil's culinary treasures.

Chapter 15: "Eternal Enchantment: Falling in Love with Brazil"

From the moment Jim set foot on Brazilian soil, he felt an inexplicable allure that whispered promises of enchantment and endless discovery. Brazil, with its kaleidoscope of landscapes, rich cultural tapestry, and warm-hearted people, has a magnetic charm that can easily transform a fleeting visit into a desire to stay forever.

Jim's journey began in the vibrant streets of Rio de Janeiro, where the rhythmic beats of samba echoed through the air, intertwining with the laughter of locals and the crashing waves along Copacabana Beach. As he explored the city's iconic landmarks, from the towering Cristo Redentor to the panoramic views atop Sugarloaf Mountain, Jim realized that each corner held a piece of Brazil's soul, inviting him to become part of its narrative.

Moving beyond the bustling metropolis, Jim found himself captivated by the Amazon Rainforest's lush embrace. The sheer biodiversity, the symphony of wildlife, and the mystical confluence of the Rio Negro and Rio Solimões left an indelible mark on his soul. The Amazon's pulse, beating in harmony with the heart of nature, whispered tales of ancient wisdom and ecological marvels that stirred Jim's adventurous spirit.

In the Northeast, the golden sands of Bahia beckoned, offering a glimpse into Brazil's Afro-Brazilian roots. Jim danced to the infectious rhythms of axé music, witnessed the vibrant colors of Festa Junina celebrations, and tasted the rich flavors of Bahian cuisine. The warmth of the locals, their infectious smiles, and the cultural richness etched into every cobblestone of Salvador made Jim feel not like a visitor but a cherished guest.

As Jim journeyed through the vast Pantanal wetlands and the captivating landscapes of Fernando de Noronha, he marveled at the wonders of Brazil's natural wonders. The Pantanal's wildlife spectacle, where jaguars and capybaras coexist harmoniously, and the pristine beaches of Fernando de Noronha, adorned with crystal-clear waters and vibrant marine life, left Jim yearning for a perpetual embrace from Brazil's natural wonders.

Culinary adventures became a gateway to Brazilian hearts, with feijoada and acarajé becoming not just dishes but expressions of a culture's love for hearty flavors and communal sharing. The street-side churrasco, the tempting açaí bowls, and the aromatic coffee ceremonies became rituals of pleasure, weaving Jim into the fabric of Brazilian social life.

Yet, beyond the geographical wonders and culinary delights, it was the warmth of the people that truly made Jim feel at home. The spontaneous friendships formed during Carnival blocos, the shared laughter at beachside soccer matches, and the genuine conversations with locals who shared stories of their lives created a sense of belonging that transcended borders.

In Brazil, time seemed to dance to its own rhythm, inviting Jim to linger in the magic of the moment. The sunsets over Ipanema painted a canvas of warm hues, and the samba-infused nights in São Paulo echoed with the promise of endless joy. The simple pleasures of a caipirinha by the beach, the camaraderie in a samba circle, and the genuine affection of strangers turned friends forged an unbreakable bond.

As Jim contemplated leaving, he found himself torn between the familiarity of his past and the magnetic pull of Brazil's embrace. The country had woven itself into the very fabric of his being, leaving an indelible mark that whispered, "Stay, for here, in

Brazil, every moment feels like forever." And in that moment of contemplation, Jim realized that, indeed, Brazil had become more than a destination—it had become a home for his heart to rest.

Chapter 16: "Feathered Stowaways: A Fowl Surprise on the Way to the Ship"

Part 1: Clucks in the Luggage

The journey to the ship took an unexpected turn as Ana and Jim, filled with anticipation for their maritime adventure, found themselves immersed in a comedy of clucks. As they cruised through the streets, the rhythmic sound of poultry percussion accompanied every twist and turn.

In the confined space of the car, Ana couldn't help but exchange curious glances with Jim. The mysterious clucking persisted, creating a comical soundtrack to their journey. Jim, with a twinkle in his eye, subtly pointed to the luggage in the backseat, raising suspicions about the source of the feathery commotion.

Upon pulling over to inspect the situation, Ana and Jim were met with an amusing revelation. The suitcases, which were meant to carry clothes and essentials for the maritime journey, had inadvertently become a cozy abode for their feathered companions, Josephina and Penelope. The luggage had transformed into a makeshift chicken coop, and the clucks of protest and curiosity resonated from within.

As they unzipped the suitcases, Ana and Jim were greeted by the sight of two chickens peeking out with a blend of bemusement and nonchalant clucking. Josephina and Penelope, seemingly unfazed by their unexpected adventure, had nestled themselves comfortably among clothes and travel essentials. The car had unwittingly become a mobile chicken caravan, and the absurdity of the situation left the couple in stitches.

The realization dawned that the sea-sized shenanigans had taken an unexpected, feathery turn. The clucks in the luggage marked the beginning of an uproarious journey with poultry passengers. Boa viagem through the clucks in the luggage, where the unforeseen addition of Josephina and Penelope turned the sea-bound adventure into a feathered escapade.

Chapter 17: Ana's British Bonanza: A Brazilian in Britain

Ana, armed with her sense of humor and a suitcase full of sunshine, embarked on a comedic escapade to the land of tea, crumpets, and peculiar weather—Britain. As she touched down on British soil, the misadventures of Ana in Britain began, promising a hilarious clash of cultures and a cascade of laughter.

Part 1: Tea Troubles and Biscuit Blunders

Ana, accustomed to the bold flavors of Brazilian coffee, found herself entangled in a labyrinth of tea choices. The seemingly simple task of ordering tea turned into a comedic spectacle as Ana navigated the intricate dance of milk-first or tea-first, perplexed by the nuances of British tea etiquette.

Her introduction to biscuits (cookies in British speak) proved equally entertaining. Accustomed to the sweetness of Brazilian treats, Ana was taken aback by the subtle flavors of digestives and custard creams. In her attempt to dunk a biscuit into tea with the grace of a Brit, she unintentionally created a "biscuit splash zone," earning amused glances from locals.

Part 2: Weather Woes and Umbrella Uproars

The unpredictable British weather became Ana's comedic nemesis. Armed with an optimistic spirit and a rainbow-colored umbrella, she ventured out, only to experience all four seasons in a single day. The umbrella, now a whimsical accessory, defied its intended purpose in the face of British gusts, turning Ana into a reluctant Mary Poppins on more than one occasion.

Ana's Brazilian wardrobe, tailored for sun-kissed days, faced an existential crisis in the British drizzle. Attempting to master the art of layering, she transformed into a walking fashion faux pas, adorned with mismatched scarves and oversized rain boots.

Part 3: Accents, Amusement, and Ana's Brazilian Charms

Ana's Brazilian charm, punctuated by infectious laughter, endeared her to the locals. Attempting British accents became a daily routine, with Ana's versions ranging from posh to comically Cockney. Conversations with locals turned into linguistic acrobatics, as Ana navigated the sea of British idioms and expressions with endearing confusion.

The locals, charmed by Ana's genuine curiosity and contagious laughter, welcomed her into the heart of British banter. Pub visits turned into comedy shows as Ana attempted to grasp the intricacies of British humor, often finding herself in fits of laughter at jokes lost in translation.

As Ana's British bonanza unfolded, the clash of cultures became a comedic symphony, with laughter bridging the gap between Brazil and Britain. The comedic tapestry of Ana's misadventures painted a picture of cultural exchange, where misunderstandings transformed into moments of shared joy, proving that laughter truly knows no borders. Boa viagem, Ana, in this British comedy of errors!

Chapter 18 Jim's Middlesbrough Marvel: Ana's Crash Course in Quirky Culture**

Jim, with a twinkle in his eye and a mischievous grin, decided to give Ana a crash course in the wonderfully quirky culture of Middlesbrough. What ensued was a comedy of cultural collisions, unexpected surprises, and, of course, plenty of laughter.

Part 1: The Mighty Boro Dialect Dilemma

Jim, proud of his Middlesbrough roots, welcomed Ana to the heart of Teesside with an enthusiastic "Howay, Ana pet!" Confused, Ana tried to decipher the mighty Boro dialect, her face a canvas of bemusement. Jim, undeterred, decided to teach her the local lingo, turning the crash course into a linguistic rollercoaster.

Ana's attempts at mastering the Teesside twang had Jim in stitches. "Pet," "bairn," and "gadgie" became the stars of the show, with Ana's interpretations transforming everyday conversations into a hilarious game of linguistic charades.

Part 2: The Parmo Paradox

Jim, eager to introduce Ana to the culinary wonders of Middlesbrough, proudly presented the "Parmo," a local delicacy that left Ana wide-eyed and slightly baffled. The concept of a chicken or pork schnitzel covered in béchamel sauce and heaps of cheese didn't align with Ana's culinary expectations.

As Ana took her first bite into the Parmo, the clash of flavors and textures created a spectacle that Jim found utterly amusing. Ana's expressions, ranging from surprise to reluctant enjoyment, turned the Parmo experience into a gastronomic comedy, leaving Jim in stitches at her delightful bewilderment.

Part 3: Football Follies and Boro Banter

No introduction to Middlesbrough culture would be complete without a visit to the Riverside Stadium. Jim, a die-hard Boro fan, took Ana to a football match, promising an immersion into the world of "Ayresome Park" chants and Boro banter.

Ana, unfamiliar with the intricacies of football fandom, found herself swept up in a sea of emotions. Jim's attempts to explain the offside rule became a slapstick comedy routine, with Ana playfully interpreting the game through exaggerated gestures and dramatic reactions.

As the final whistle blew, Jim and Ana, surrounded by passionate Boro fans, joined in the post-match banter. Ana's attempts at football-themed quips left Jim in fits of laughter, turning the football experience into a joyful celebration of cultural exchange.

In the end, Jim's Middlesbrough marvel became a delightful comedy of cultural collisions, with Ana embracing the quirks and charms of Teesside with infectious laughter. The clash of Brazilian and Boro cultures turned into a cultural comedy, proving that the heart of humor transcends geographical borders. Boa viagem, Ana, in this laughter-filled journey through Middlesbrough's unique tapestry of culture!

Chapter 19: Ana's British Family Fiesta: Navigating In-Laws, Laughter, and the Quirks of a British Clan

Tea Time

Tea time at Anne's was like entering a refined comedy club, where etiquette and hilarity shared the stage. Ana, with her Brazilian exuberance, approached the ritual of afternoon tea with the zest of a carnival. Anne, her mother-in-law, a paragon of British sophistication, observed Ana's animated attempts to balance the delicate china cups and saucers with amusement. As Ana sipped her tea, a bemused expression played on her face as if she'd just discovered a new flavor in the cosmic tea universe. Anne, with a twinkle in her eye, offered scones, guiding Ana through the intricate dance of spreading clotted cream and jam. The clinking of teaspoons harmonized with Ana's contagious laughter, turning tea time into a delightful blend of British charm and Brazilian vivacity. Boa viagem through the whimsical world of tea, Ana, where laughter and elegance danced gracefully on the delicate notes of a teacup symphony!

Having a pint

One evening at the local pub, Ana found herself in the spirited company of Jim's friends, Androo and Singh. The trio, representing a cultural kaleidoscope, transformed the pub into a laughter-filled stage. Androo, with his charming Yorkshire accent, regaled Ana with tales of Middlesbrough's quirks, while Singh, with his impeccable sense of humor, sprinkled the conversation with Punjabi punchlines. As pints were raised and laughter echoed through the pub, Ana, caught in the crossfire of Yorkshire wit and Punjabi banter, contributed her own brand of Brazilian charm. Singh attempted a Brazilian samba move, Androo mimicked a Brazilian carnival queen, and Ana reciprocated with a Bollywood-style twirl. The pub, now a global comedy stage, witnessed a cultural mashup of epic proportions, proving that in the realm of laughter, borders blurred, and camaraderie knew no cultural bounds. Boa viagem, Ana, through the uproarious pub tales with Androo and Singh!

At Nana's house

A visit to Nana's house for Ana and Jim was like stepping into a whimsical realm of delightful chaos. The air was infused with the sweet scent of Nana's renowned Victoria Sponge cake, a culinary masterpiece that held the secrets of generations. Ana, eager to partake in the family tradition, offered her assistance, but Nana, with a playful twinkle in her eye, subjected her to a taste test of epic proportions. Ana's animated reactions to each forkful turned the kitchen into a comedy show, with Jim and Nana playing the roles of amused spectators.

As the laughter-filled cake sampling continued, Nana decided to add an unexpected twist â€" a liberal dash of her favorite brandy. The combination of brandy-laced cake and Ana's theatrical taste-testing sent the trio into fits of giggles, turning the kitchen into a stage for culinary comedy.

Amidst the delightful chaos, Jim couldn't help but share anecdotes of his marine engineer grandad, whose memories were as rich as the brandy in Nana's cake. The kitchen became a time machine, transporting them to an era where grandad's nautical tales collided with Ana's Brazilian flair and Nana's timeless recipes.

And so, in Nana's kitchen, surrounded by the intoxicating aroma of cake and the echoes of grandad's seafaring stories, Ana and Jim found themselves immersed in a unique blend of family traditions, culinary capers, and laughter that transcended generations. Boa viagem through the comical culinary journey, Ana and Jim, in the heart of Nana's kitchen time warp!

With sisters's

A visit to the sisters-in-law's house, hosted by the dynamic duo Nicola and Clare, turned into a laughter-infused expedition for Ana and Jim. The evening started innocently enough, but as the bottles clinked and the wine flowed, the comedic chaos unfolded. The house, already bustling with the energy of three hyperactive nephews and a pack of spirited dogs, became a playground for unbridled hilarity.

Ana and Jim, with their inhibitions steadily drowned in the sea of spirits, found themselves in the midst of a tipsy symphony. Attempts to engage in adult conversations were repeatedly interrupted by the chaos orchestrated by the three nephews, who seemed to have discovered a newfound passion for interpretative dance.

The dogs, caught in the crossfire of the tipsy tumult, joined the festivities, creating a canine conga line that had everyone in splits. Amidst the laughter, Ana attempted to match the energy of the hyperactive nephews, turning the living room into an impromptu dance floor.

As the night wore on, and the comedy of errors reached its peak, Nicola and Clare, adept at managing the madness, decided to call it a night. Ana and Jim, still in fits of giggles, bid farewell to the chaotic carnival at the sisters-in-law's house, promising to return for another round of nephews, dogs, and intoxicating laughter. Boa viagem through the tipsy tales, Ana and Jim, in the heart of the sisters-in-law's house of mirth!

20. The Celestial Cheers: Jim's Heavenly Summons and Divine Drinks**

As the final part of the earthly adventure unfolded, a cosmic commotion stirred in the celestial realm. Angels, celestial beings, and a mischievous spirit named Jim gathered for a heavenly fiesta. It was time for Jim's grand summons to the ethereal plane, but this celestial affair had a twist—it came complete with divine drinks, heavenly hilarity, and a celestial pub that rivaled the best on Earth.

Part 1: Jim's Angelic Summons

The cosmic comedy kicked off with the celestial announcement of Jim's grand summons. Angels, clad in laughter-infused robes, formed a celestial conga line, dancing their way to Earth to bring Jim back to the heavenly realm. Laughter echoed through the cosmos as Jim, now a celestial jester, joined the celestial parade with a wink and a cheeky grin.

As the angels surrounded Jim, preparing for his ascension, he negotiated for a brief earthly detour. "Just one more round of laughter," he pleaded, and the heavenly host, enchanted by Jim's earthly humor, agreed. The celestial comedy club was born, and the divine drinks flowed like laughter in the cosmic wind.

Part 2: Heaven's Hilarious Hops and Angelic Ales

In the celestial pub, aptly named "Divine Drunkenness," heavenly beers and wines flowed like stardust from celestial taps. Jim, now the honorary bartender, served up laughter-infused ales and angelic brews with a splash of cosmic humor. The angels, accustomed to celestial sobriety, indulged in the heavenly elixirs, their laughter creating celestial waves that rippled through the heavens.

As the heavenly patrons clinked celestial glasses, Jim regaled them with tales of his earthly adventures. The mischievous spirit, now a cosmic comedian, had the angels in stitches with anecdotes of phantom pranks, linguistic capoeira, and the Great Caipirinha Challenge. Laughter, the universal language, echoed through the heavenly pub, creating an atmosphere of joy that transcended the boundaries of the earthly and the celestial.

Part 3: A Cosmic Toast to Laughter Eternal

As the laughter in heaven reached its celestial climax, the angels, now honorary members of the earthly linguistic adventure, raised their glasses in a cosmic toast. Jim, with a twinkle in his eye, proposed a final toast to "laughter eternal." The heavenly patrons, now in high spirits, clinked their glasses, and celestial laughter reverberated through the cosmos.

With a celestial sigh, Jim bid his earthly companions farewell, promising that the echoes of laughter would linger in the heavens forever. The cosmic comedy club, now a celestial landmark, became a beacon of joy for angels and celestial beings alike. As Jim ascended to the celestial realms, the laughter-infused stardust of Earth followed him, creating a celestial comet that would forever light up the cosmic expanse.

And so, as the heavenly fiesta continued in the celestial pub, Jim, the mischievous spirit turned cosmic comedian, became a legend among angels. The laughter, the drinks, and the joy of the earthly linguistic adventure became a celestial memory, eternally celebrated in the laughter-filled halls of heaven. Boa viagem, Jim, boa viagem!

Chapter 21

The Tapestry of Emotion

In the quiet moments of the night, Ana found herself sitting by the window, gazing at the stars that adorned the sky like twinkling memories. The room was filled with the hushed symphony of sorrow and the soft echoes of laughter that lingered in the corners of her heart. The absence of her best friend and husband, James, left an indescribable void.

Grief, like a heavy fog, settled around her. The weight of loss pressed against her chest, making it hard to breathe. The laughter they once shared echoed in her mind, a sweet melody that now carried a poignant note of absence. The love they built together was like a thread woven into the fabric of her life, and James's departure had left an unraveling tapestry of emotions.

Ana clutched the old photo album in her hands, flipping through the pages that told the story of their journey. Pictures captured moments of joy, love, and shared laughter. A tear traced the outline of her cheek as she lingered on the images that seemed to radiate warmth, a warmth that now felt distant.

In the quiet of the night, she whispered words that only the stars could hear – messages of love and longing, a conversation carried on the wings of grief. The room became a sacred space where memories were both a source of comfort and an ache that throbbed with the absence of James's laughter.

Yet, as Ana sat there in the embrace of solitude, she realized that love was an everlasting flame that could not be extinguished by the winds of grief. James may no longer be physically present, but his love lingered in the very air she breathed. It was in the familiar scent of their shared spaces, the remnants of laughter embedded in the walls, and the gentle touch of memories that painted the room.

In the quiet acceptance of missing her best husband, Ana felt a bittersweet dance of emotions. Love and grief, laughter and sorrow – they were threads in the intricate tapestry of life. As she closed the photo album, she knew that the chapters of their story weren't confined to the past. Instead, they were the foundation of the love that would continue to unfold, a story that transcended the boundaries of time and space

Chapter 22

Echoes Across Continents

Ana stood at the edge of the Cliffs of Moher, the winds carrying whispers of memories that danced around her like ethereal spirits. The rugged cliffs stretched as far as the eye could see, mirroring the vastness of the love she once shared with James. As she closed her eyes, the rolling waves below seemed to echo the laughter they had shared in faraway lands.

The journey had begun with a simple promise – to explore the world hand in hand. James, her adventurous soulmate, had a knack for turning every destination into a canvas where they painted the hues of their shared experiences. From the bustling markets of Marrakech to the serene temples of Kyoto, they had left traces of their love on the map of the world.

Ana's fingers traced the pages of her travel journal, each entry a vivid snapshot of their escapades. In Paris, they had locked a padlock on the Pont des Arts, symbolizing their unbreakable bond. In the heart of the Amazon rainforest, they had marveled at the kaleidoscope of colors that nature had woven together.

But as she traveled alone now, Ana realized that the memories weren't confined to the places they had visited; they were embedded in the very essence of her being. Every cobblestone street, every mountain vista, and every sunset painted across foreign skies carried the imprint of their shared adventures.

In the bustling streets of Tokyo, Ana could almost hear James's laughter as they navigated the maze of neon lights and bustling crowds. The aroma of street food in Bangkok transported her back to the evenings they spent huddled together, savoring local delicacies under the glittering lanterns.

As she stood beneath the Northern Lights in Iceland, Ana felt a connection that transcended the physical realm. The vibrant dance of colors in the night sky mirrored the kaleidoscope of emotions within her. James may no longer be beside her, but the echoes of their shared laughter resonated across continents, creating a tapestry of memories that spanned the globe.

With each step, Ana embraced the bittersweet truth that her solo travels were a continuation of the journey they had started together. Her heart, though heavy with the absence of James, was also lifted by the joyous recollections of a life well-lived. The world became a living memorial, each landmark a testament to a love that transcended borders and time.

And so, with a heart full of gratitude and a suitcase laden with memories, Ana continued to explore the world, carrying James's spirit with her. The wind whispered tales of love, and as she watched the sunset over the Cliffs of Moher, she felt an undeniable connection to the man who had been her greatest adventure.

Final

Ticket to Laughter

Ana found herself in a peculiar waiting room, adorned with fluffy clouds and an ethereal glow. Confused, she looked around, trying to make sense of her surroundings.

"Hello, Ana!" a familiar voice chimed, and there, standing amidst the celestial mist, was none other than Jim – her beloved husband who had departed from the earthly plane before her.

"Jim! Is this... heaven?" Ana asked, a mix of astonishment and amusement coloring her voice.

Jim nodded, grinning from ear to ear. "Yep! Welcome to the Departure Lounge for the next leg of our journey."

"Departure Lounge? Are we catching a flight to eternity or something?" Ana chuckled, eyeing the fluffy clouds suspiciously.

Jim winked. "Not quite, my love. We're catching a flight around the celestial wonders! I've been exploring the heavenly locales, and I thought, why not plan a grand adventure together?"

Ana burst into laughter. "You mean we get to travel even after we're... you know, up here?"

Jim nodded enthusiastically. "Absolutely! I've secured us the best seats on the Cosmic Express. We'll be zipping through galaxies, taking pit stops at nebulas, and maybe even trying out some zero-gravity stunts!"

Ana couldn't contain her laughter. "You've really outdone yourself, Jim! I never thought the afterlife came with a travel itinerary."

Jim shrugged playfully. "Heaven's got to keep up with the times, you know? So, what do you say, ready for the grand tour of the great beyond?"

Ana pretended to ponder, tapping her chin. "Well, I was planning on exploring the earthly wonders a bit more, but how can I resist a cosmic adventure with you? Let's do it!"

And so, in the heavenly Departure Lounge, Ana and Jim awaited their celestial departure, giddy with anticipation. As they shared laughter and traded jokes, it became clear that even in the afterlife, their love was an everlasting journey filled with unexpected detours and cosmic delights.

Little did they know that their next adventure would be the most extraordinary one yet, taking them to places where the stars themselves became their travel companions. The Departure Lounge may have been unconventional, but Ana and Jim were ready for the laughter-filled escapade that awaited them in the vast expanse of the universe.

About The Author

Ana Paula T. Bassani Da Silva Mcculloch

Ana Paula's life was a tapestry of adventures woven alongside her beloved husband, Jim, a skilled marine engineer. Together, they embarked on a journey that spanned the globe, navigating oceans and exploring the farthest reaches of seven continents. Their love story unfolded against the backdrop of exotic landscapes and diverse cultures, creating a kaleidoscope of shared experiences.

Tragedy struck when Jim, the anchor of Ana's world, passed away unexpectedly. Left with a heart heavy with grief, Ana faced a crossroads, unsure of how to navigate the vast seas of life alone. However, fueled by the indomitable spirit they had cultivated together, Ana chose not to let the final chapter of their adventure be defined by sorrow.

As a widowed young woman, Ana carried the memories of their travels like precious treasures, using them as a compass to guide her forward. The echoes of Jim's laughter resonated in the wind as Ana continued their explorations, discovering new horizons and embracing the unknown with resilience and courage.

In this poignant tale of love, loss, and resilience, Ana Paula emerges as a beacon of strength, proving that even after the departure of a soulmate, the journey of life continues. With each step, Ana weaves new threads into the tapestry of her existence, honoring Jim's memory while forging her path through the uncharted waters of a changed world. The story encapsulates the enduring power of love, the transformative nature of grief, and the possibility of finding joy in unexpected places even after bidding farewell to a cherished travel companion.

Printed in Great Britain
by Amazon

36917539R00051